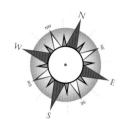

HIKING

FOR

BEGINNERS

Julian Tippett

CAXTON EDITIONS

First published and distributed in the UK in 1999 by:
Caxton Editions
16 Connaught Street
Marble Arch
London W2 2AF

ISBN: 1-84067-091-6

This is a MARS book

Edited, designed and produced by Haldane Mason, London

Printed in China

Acknowledgements
Art Director: Ron Samuels
Editorial Director: Sydney Francis
Editor: Jane Ellis
Design: Sarah Collins
Artwork: Stephen Dew, Julian Tippett

Picture Acknowledgements
Photographs reproduced with kind permission of: Sydney Francis 4, 7, 8, 10, 12, 20, 28, 30, 46, 54, 61; Blacks Outdoor Suppliers 14, 50, 63; © Ordnance Survey Crown Copyright Licence No. MC 99/47 11; The Meteorological Office and the *Guardian* 13; Julian Tippett 31, 42; Rex Features Limited 52.
Every has been made to trace copyright holders and we apologize in advance for any unintentional omissions. We would be pleased to insert the appropriate acknowledgement in any subsequent edition of this publication.

Special thanks to:

Contents

Introduction

Few activities offer more
pleasure than hiking: the
view over a mountain lake,
a glimpse of a deer picking
its way over moss-clad
stones, that wonderful
physical exhaustion after a
day on the trail, and, above
all, the challenge of
preparing for and executing a
successful expedition.

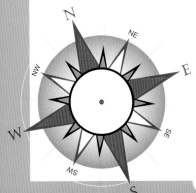

As with any worthwhile endeavour, there is much to learn, but even with a minimum of knowledge you can soon get out on to easy trails and start to accumulate that all-important experience. The purpose of this book, together with the compass, is to help you get into the wide outdoors easily and safely.

If you are keen to navigate well, you will need to buy a hiking compass with a baseplate (see page 37).

This book aims to cover the essential knowledge and techniques of hiking in enough depth to get a beginner on the trail safely. But these trails (or off-path routes) must be relatively easy; the book does not advise on hikes in hazardous or high terrain, poor weather, winter conditions, or on backpacking expeditions. Those going out for the first time should cut their teeth on short, simple day hikes when the weather forecast is

Hiking or the act of putting one foot in front of another is defined in many ways:

UK –	*walking or rambling*
USA –	*trekking*
Australia –	*bushwalking or trekking*
NZ –	*tramping*

good, and work up to longer, more demanding routes by stages.

You will learn most from the hikes themselves. The discomfort resulting from mistakes, such as forgetting your waterproof or taking a wrong turning, teaches more than any book can. You will gradually build up your knowledge, and as you branch into new hiking localities, your map library will expand. Outdoor magazines can be a treasure chest of useful advice and ideas.

Another source of experienced help is your local hiking club, which might be called a rambling, backpacking or long-distance walking club. You should be able to find out the name of the secretary, your foothold into the club, from your local library or information centre. Most such clubs organize group hikes and other ways of meeting and learning from the 'old hands', and you might team up there with other kindred spirits to launch your own expeditions.

Conservation

The deeper into the countryside a hike goes, the better it becomes. But as more people start to enjoy nature, the greater the risk they will destroy the very thing that attracts them. Wilder parts belong to flora and fauna. Hikers are uninvited guests who need to be on their best behaviour and avoid thoughtless actions that could result in litter, damage or even fires. Find out about local advice on disposal of human waste, and observe it strictly. Take all your litter home with you. The motto is 'take nothing but photographs, leave nothing but footprints.'

Less wild countryside, just as attractive to walk in, is usually the domain of farmers. Here too walkers are guests who must take care – keeping gates shut, dogs under control, and avoiding damage to crops or water supplies – in short, to be thoughtful and sensitive about their behaviour.

Always make sure that you leave the country as you found it – litter-free and unpolluted.

Emergencies

With care and experience, accidents are unlikely. However, if you go hiking often, there is a possibility that something could go wrong and prove serious enough to call the emergency services into action. Serious hiking expeditions carry risk. It is crucial that all those who undertake such expeditions are aware of and accept the risks, and take responsibility for their actions. Emergencies and first-aid procedures are covered in Chapter 6.

Warning

The safety advice in this book holds good for most hiking localities. However, in some regions particular dangers and risks can mean that different safety rules apply. You are strongly advised to obtain the safety advice that applies to your own locality before setting out.

Chapter One

Preparing for your hike

Whether a local afternoon stroll or a demanding full-day hike in difficult terrain, your outing will be all the better for attentive planning. The more care and thought you put into preparing for the hike, the more likely you are to enjoy it.

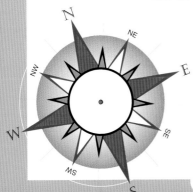

The process of choosing a suitable route from the map is dealt with later. But you must also think about where to get your maps, what equipment to take, who will make up your party, the weather. Sort these things out, and you can be confident of a pleasant and trouble-free outing.

Where to hike

Which are the best places to hike will always be a matter of personal taste. If you are starting out, you might not know what possibilities exist, which means having to get down to some detective work. Outdoor magazines will give valuable information, as will talking to friends and contacts in the local hiking club. Look out for local hiking guide books. At first you should stick to the more popular areas, as here the trails will be clearly marked and you are more likely to find better maps. Less-frequented, wilder country can wait until you are more experienced.

Get some experience before tackling more rugged countryside, especially if you are hiking abroad in unfamiliar terrain and conditions.

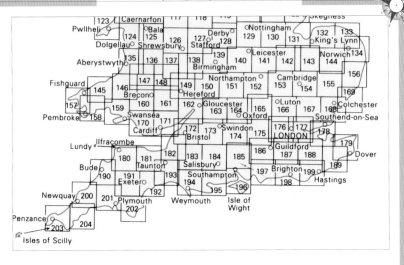

An index such as this one will give details of all the maps in a series.

Getting maps

Maps can be found in bookshops and outdoor equipment specialist stores, whose sales staff are often a mine of information. The best scales for walking are between 1:25,000 and 1:62,500, tending toward the lower number (i.e. larger scale) if your area has many trails and much detail. To understand scale, see page 25. The best way to choose a map is first to look on any map's cover for an index of all maps in the series, or ask for the separate index. Choose from this what you think is the right map for your hike area, but then be sure to check its coverage by looking into the map itself. Often a map publisher will supply on request a more detailed index than the one on the cover.

To go with the map, you need a transparent map case to protect it. The case will carry the map folded to reveal the area of your hike, saving time each time you stop to navigate. If your map case is not waterproof, carry a clear plastic bag to put the map in (inside the case) for when it rains, or you could have an expensive soggy mess at the end of the day. Check you have your compass and whistle to go with the map; a notebook and pen can sometimes come in handy.

Permission for access

If you have chosen a hiking area you know is popular, you will be pretty sure you are permitted to walk there without more ado. However, in certain areas in some countries, you need to check with park authorities whether the trail you want to use allows only limited numbers and you have to book. If you are intending to go off-trail, check whether back-country permits are needed. In some localities all hiking must follow recognized trails and no back-country access is permitted.

Size of party

Until you understand the risks involved, it is unwise to hike alone, and besides it's much more fun to go with companions. If your hike will be in any way challenging, you must accept the possibility of an accident, which means a minimum of three people in the party – one to go for help and one to stay with the injured person. Four would be better, allowing two to go for help. Everyone needs to be fit enough for the walk that is planned, and should fully understand and accept what is involved.

If the hike involves steep hills or crossing rivers, it is essential that all members of the party are fit enough to undertake it.

Weather

WET and windy in Scotland and Northern Ireland with snow on the mountains. Some rain in Wales, and western England. Drier elsewhere. **Channel Is, Cent S & SE England, London, E Anglia, Lincs:** Starting cold but bright. Cloudier later. A moderate westerly wind. Max temp 5-8C (41-46F). Tonight, clear spells. Min temp 3-5C (37-41F). **Midlands:** Sunny spells and showers this morning. Dull and wet this afternoon. A moderate westerly wind. Max temp 5-8C (41-46F). Tonight, becoming dry. Min temp 3-4C (37-39F). **SW & NW England, Wales,**

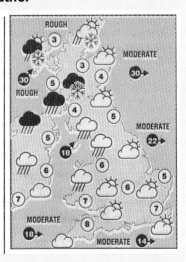

Weather charts and forecasts are provided by the Meteorological Office and published in most national and local newspapers.

A hike can change amazingly quickly from a carefree stroll in glorious sunny weather to a demanding ordeal if the rain starts to pour and mist rolls down. The quality and availability of weather forecasts can vary widely from place to place. If you do not have access to a reliable forecast, you need to know what is the worst possible weather that you could expect to encounter at that time of year, and be prepared for it.

If good weather forecasts are available, then it pays to get hold of them, and to understand them, as they can influence your choice of clothing, route, or the emergency plans you formulate 'just in case'. It's worth getting a suitable book to improve your weather knowledge.

The crucial factors to look for are: temperature, wind speed and direction, and whether there will be rain or snow, or sunshine. The most common bad weather combinations that can give high chill factors are wind and low temperature, or wind and rain. If anything, the latter is more serious, needing all your weather-proof clothing. A snow storm could result in 'white out', the most dangerous condition of all.

Chapter Two

Equipment

This chapter aims to help you to select the type of gear best suited to your walking conditions, and to provide a checklist on what to take on the hike. A good weather forecast can help with some decisions; others will be settled by experience.

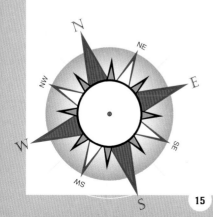

Clothing

First-time hikers are often astonished at the difference in weather between low and high ground. People can be sunbathing at the foot of a modest-sized mountain, while walkers on its summit are putting on all their winter woollies. This is partly an effect of altitude, partly that mountains attract bad weather. Hikers must expect the weather to do its worst.

Warm clothing such as a fleece or pullover is essential. Remember that many light layers are easier to adjust than a single thick one. Always take enough spare clothing to be able to cope with the worst weather you could encounter, or to keep warm during an enforced stay outdoors.

You will need a waterproof and windproof layer too – jacket and overtrousers. (Avoid jeans as they absorb vast quantities of water and go cold and stiff.) Garments made from modern breathable fabrics, which keep the rain out but allow your perspiration to escape, will keep both rain and wind at bay. A good jacket will have a comfortable hood, big enough to cover your hat, map and other pockets, and a flap to cover the zip. Get one large enough to wear over all your winter clothing. Don't forget gloves and hat; you will lose heat faster from your head than from any other part of the body.

Mountain sun burns strongly, so take some simple precautions to ensure that you are adequately protected against it: wear a hat, suitable clothing, and a high-factor sunblock cream.

Footwear

Once the trail gets rough, boots become a necessity. They need not be expensive, but make certain they are robust, comfortable and have a cleated sole. When making your purchase, take along the thick socks you will be wearing, and try the boots on with these.

Make sure you stay warm and dry in the worst weather conditions.

Comfortable boots are essential to enjoy your hike.

Take time walking about the shop to check their comfort. Do they have enough room for your toes when coming downhill? Do they feel tight anywhere?

Fabric boots are becoming popular and generally do a good job. However, if you are going to be walking a lot in marshy terrain or in winter, good leather boots will always be better. Whichever type of boot you choose, always wear thick, comfortable socks.

Backpacks

A rucksack is essential; 35 litres (2,100 cubic in.) is a good size for a long day hike. If you want to go on backpacking expeditions or demanding day hikes in back-country, then you will need one of 45 litres (2,700 cubic in.) and upwards. Assuming that you will be carrying a reasonably sized load, make certain the rucksack has a stiffened back and a padded waistbelt that fits your waist. Careful adjustment of the straps on this type of rucksack makes carrying the load much easier by transferring the weight largely from the shoulders to hips.

When packing a large load into a rucksack, put the heavier items close to your back and as near the top as possible, to help your balance when walking. No rucksack is waterproof, so if there is any likelihood of rain, you could either pack vulnerable kit in plastic bags before stowing them in the rucksack, or line your rucksack with plastic bin-liners.

When putting on a rucksack, first pull the waistband firm on the hips, then adjust the shoulder straps until they are comfortably tight.

Food and water

Besides your day's picnic, emergency rations should be carried in case you are forced to spend much longer on your hike than planned, even an enforced night out. The best sort is concentrated high-energy food, such as dried fruit, biscuits, chocolate and candies.

It is crucial to take enough to drink. (This should be of a strictly non-alcoholic variety as alcohol increases dehydration!) On a hot day you may need to drink two or three litres of water to replace the amount of fluid lost from your body: without this your performance will suffer. You can buy special drinking bottles, but any

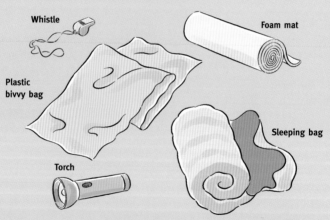

Survival gear

Whistle

Foam mat

Plastic bivvy bag

Sleeping bag

Torch

Other survival gear to consider (besides your whistle) are first-aid kit, torch (plus spare batteries), an insulation mat, and for a back-country winter hike – a sleeping-bag.

As anyone doing a hike runs the risk, however remote, of being benighted, or of becoming immobilized by an accident, it is wise for each hiker to carry a bivvy (bivouac) bag – a stout plastic bag about two metres long, big enough to accommodate fully a hiker with all clothing on. In wet or cold conditions, a bivvy bag increases the chances of preventing body temperature dropping to dangerous levels while help is summoned or an enforced night out is endured in bad conditions.

empty plastic drinks bottle with a good screw cap will do fine.

Beware filling your bottles from mountain streams, unless you are absolutely certain they are free from pollution. In North America and New Zealand you should take into account that any stream could carry the bacterial infection *giardia*, which means that water there would have to be purified by special tablets or by boiling, before you could drink it.

Mobile phones and GPS

These electronic gizmos now have a place in outdoor activity, but need to viewed with some caution. Their roles differ, as do hikers' attitudes to them.

Mobile phone

It is assumed here that the only purpose for taking one on a hike is as a means of summoning help in an emergency, not to keep up with the gossip! A number of incidents are on record where a mobile phone has played an invaluable part in getting the rescue services quickly to a casualty, but hikers must understand that they cannot always be relied on. Since the phone's transmitter is inherently weak, it depends on a full network of ground stations that may be scarce in back-country regions.

If you are hiking on remote trails, the signal might not get through, just when you need it most, so you must always be ready with the traditional emergency procedures.

GPS

The Global Positioning System comprises a hand-held device that interprets signals from a number of satellites orbiting the earth to give a read-out defining the user's current position, accurate to about 100 metres. This device has on a number of occasions enabled hikers to locate themselves in poor visibility, such that they could find their way out of trouble and off the hill. These systems also have many professional uses.

Although a GPS might seem to be the answer to every hiker's prayer, it does have snags and this means you still need to know how to navigate. It only defines position, and then only if the user is well practised and has a map with a grid compatible with the machine's read-out. To find the right direction to go from your location defined by the GPS still needs all your map-reading skills. A GPS requires a frequent supply of fresh batteries for good performance and, fun though it is to own, it has little value if your hiking is confined to well-marked trails.

Chapter Three

Reading a map

A map is the bird's eye view of a part of the earth's surface represented on a flat sheet of paper. There's an amazing amount of detail in a map and it is worth making the effort to learn how to find it!

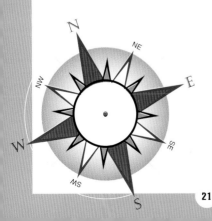

Symbols

A true bird's-eye view, as in an aerial photograph, would show every tree and bush, in fact everything that's there, but in reality important details like tracks and buildings can often get lost. The map, on the other hand, emphasizes the information that is of interest to its readers. To make it clear, maps use easily understood symbols, like a code, to represent the objects to be found on the ground. And each symbol is located in its proper place on the map. As with any code, it helps to learn the symbols on the particular map you are using for your hike, and for this reason each map has a key printed in its margin. See the simple key here which we shall use for the maps in this booklet. Your hiking map will show many more types of object than we use here, such as power lines, different types of forest, county boundaries, etc.

It pays to learn the code to the map key.

Comparing map with ground

Already we can look at a simple piece of countryside and the map that portrays it. One of the map-reading tasks you will often do is to compare the map with the countryside, to check where you are or to work out the next part of route to walk. Try this out by comparing the surroundings of Rutter's Farm (opposite) with the corresponding map. Immediately you encounter a problem – while the map gives a bird's-eye view, your own view, being ground based, is quite different. Your view is distorted: near things look large and distant objects small, whereas on the map they are shown in scale based on the actual size.

Furthermore, many of the objects on the map, which you think you should be able to see, are hidden, possibly by a forest or tucked away behind a hill. Every map-reader just has to practise to acquire the knack of relating what's on the ground to what is in the map.

Another quirk is that the map is a flat sheet of paper, whereas the ground it represents is anything but this, with hills, peaks and valleys.

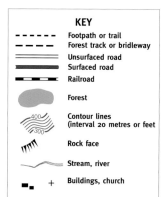

KEY

– – – – –	Footpath or trail
– – – –	Forest track or bridleway
=====	Unsurfaced road
▬▬▬▬▬	Surfaced road
■▬■▬■	Railroad
⬤	Forest
〰400〰 〰300〰	Contour lines (interval 20 metres or feet
⋀⋀⋀	Rock face
〰〰	Stream, river
▬∎ +	Buildings, church

The surroundings of Rutter's Farm.

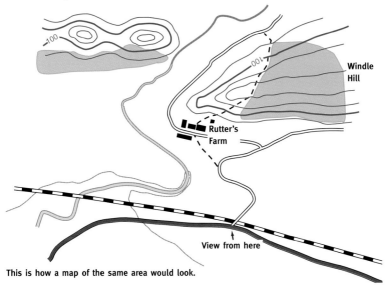

Windle
Hill

Rutter's
Farm

View from here

This is how a map of the same area would look.

Over the years map-makers have used many devices such as hill-shading and coloured layers to portray on the map what is known as 'relief'. Nowadays almost all maps use squiggly brown lines, contours, to show the folds of the earth. These have the advantage of great precision, but with the drawback that they take some practice to get used to. They are examined in some detail on pages 26–32.

Reference grid

Many hiking maps are covered by a grid of fine squares, part of a national referencing system (UK: National Grid). There will be an explanation of how it works in the map margin. Such a grid helps when using the compass by providing a reference to north from anywhere on the map. What's more, if you know the size of each square, the grid helps you judge distances (in the UK they are 1 kilometre across).

Administrative boundaries

One set of symbols to learn that you will probably never use is that of administrative boundaries (like counties). You need to be able to recognize these to avoid confusing them with paths and trying to walk along their line, or you could find yourself crashing through some very prickly terrain!

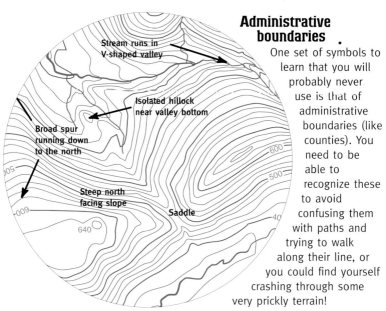

Stream runs in V-shaped valley

Isolated hillock near valley bottom

Broad spur running down to the north

Steep north facing slope

Saddle

600

500

640

Scale

An obvious feature of any map is that it is only a fraction the size of the land it represents, but how much smaller is it? It is important to understand 'scale', as it is known, as it will help you to measure distances on the map and on the ground, and will give precision to map-reading and planning. Each map is drawn to particular scale, such as 1:25,000, which can be found by looking into the margin of the map. In practice, this means that: one centimetre (or inch) on the map represents 25,000 centimetres (or inches) on the ground.

Maps are covered by a grid of fine squares. In the UK the distance between each line is one kilometre.

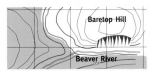

Baretop Hill

Beaver River

Since 25,000 cm is 250 metres, or a quarter kilometre, then 4 cm represents 1 km. In miles and inches, there are 2.5 inches to the mile. For the two most popular scales for walkers, the following applies:

Scale	Metric	Imperial
1:25,000	1 km = 4 cm on the map	1 mile = 2.5 inches
1:50,000	1 km = 2 cm on the map	1 mile = 1.25 inches

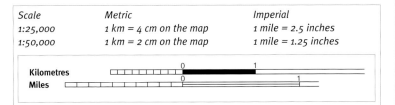

Kilometres

Miles

Similar calculations can be done on any scale, the most common other ones for hikers being 1:24,000 and 1:62,500. You can measure distances in miles and kilometres against the scale bar on the map.

How does all this help in practice? When planning your day's hike, you can make an essential check that the hike is not too long and is within the capability of your party. Suppose you have worked out a route on a 1:25,000 map and you find that a string laid along the wiggles of the line of the route stretches out to a length of 34 cm. Each 4 cm represents 1 km. Thus you know that the walk will be 8.5 km long.

Contours

The most difficult part of map-reading for most people is getting to understand contours. Amazingly, these twisty lines can be read so as to let you visualize the shape of the countryside, even down to little gullies and hillocks. At first, the contours on your hiking map will seem just a jumble of lines, but it pays to put real effort into understanding them and acquiring the knack of 'seeing' the lie of the land from the map in three dimensions. This ability gives much pleasure, and reveals many useful clues for navigating your route.

In particular the capacity to read contours can help you to:

● Pinpoint your position by comparing the land shapes near you with the features shown on the map.
● Use land features to follow when planning the next leg of your hike in back-country.
● 'Read' the scenery from a map when getting to know a new hiking area.
● Pick walks with the best views by recognizing paths that go over hills.
● Guard against following routes that are too steep to walk safely.

Rules for contours

Contours on the map obey a number of rules:

● Each contour lies at a specific number of metres (or feet) above sea-level.

● Each one is spaced vertically a certain distance from its upper and lower neighbours: the 'contour interval'. The maps in this book use 20 metres; you will need to inspect the margin of your hiking map to discover the interval it employs.

● Every fifth contour is a thicker 'index' contour, which helps to read them more easily.

● Where the map-maker has space, he numbers a contour line with its height. Usually, the numbers are placed so that their upper edge points uphill, which explains why sometimes they are printed upside down.

● Spot heights of certain locations are shown, often the tops of hills. Some of these are known as trigonometrical (trig) points.

How contours are drawn
on a map

A contour traces an imaginary line on the ground that is always level; if you walked along a contour, you would *neither climb nor descend, even on a hillside, as you would be walking around the hill.*

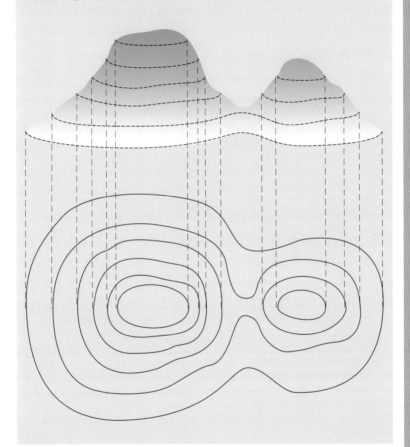

Here now are a few points to bear in mind when interpreting contours:

● if a contour makes a complete ring with no ring inside, it's the top of a hill – keep an eye open for these.

● the spacing of contours defines the steepness of slope – close together if steep and widely spaced if gentle.

● the land is often folded into a series of valleys, separated by spurs between them. The contour patterns of valleys and spurs often look similar. To tell them apart:

– look for streams, obviously at the bottom of the valleys.
– the contours make a series of 'V's (or sometimes 'U's). If the 'V's point uphill, it's a valley; if downhill, a spur.

Study the map of a hilly area shown on page 32, which highlights some of these features. Also look at page 29 and on the following pages at the photographs and the corresponding maps of convex and concave slopes, a saddle and a ridge, to compare some common land shapes with their contour patterns.

Convex slopes are steeper at the bottom, so the contours are closer at the bottom of the slope.

As concave slopes are steepest at the top, contours are closer together at the top.

Reading the scenery

One of the great pleasures awaiting you is when you open up the map of a new hiking area to get a feel for what the countryside is like to walk in and start to plan some hikes. By putting to work your newly won contour knowledge, you can enrich this process by reading the landscape – where will the best views be? Which paths look most interesting? Here are some hints:

● Scan the map for contour heights and spot heights – form an impression of where the high and low areas are.

● Look for ring contours to fix the lines of hills.

● Rivers and streams are the tell-tale sign of valleys.

● Areas with many contours close together signify steep slopes, a sign of good walking and views.

● Rock markings and very close contours warn about steep slopes.

... is an example of a convex slope (in the middle of the photo).

Convex slope

400

300

Concave slope, with ridge above it.

Ridge

Concave slope

500

400

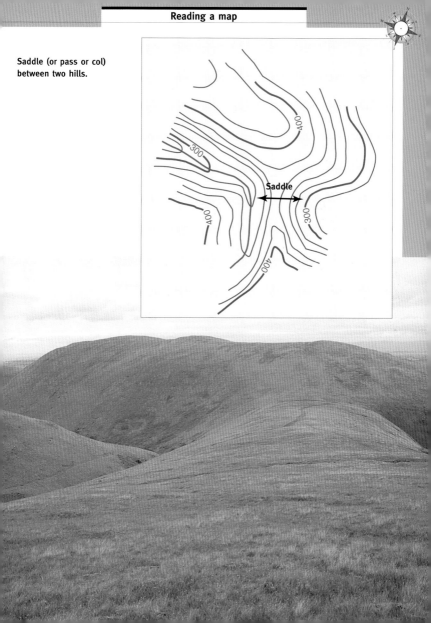

Saddle (or pass or col) between two hills.

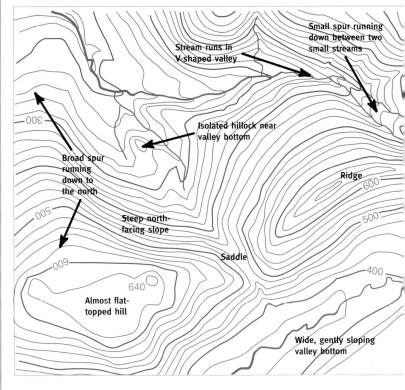

Small spur running down between two small streams

Stream runs in V-shaped valley

Isolated hillock near valley bottom

Broad spur running down to the north

300

Ridge

600

600

Steep north-facing slope

500

Saddle

009

640

400

Almost flat-topped hill

Wide, gently sloping valley bottom

This hilly area shows some common land shapes (see page 28).

Navigating on the trail

Now that you know the basics of maps, you are ready to start navigating a route for real. Obviously it's best to start with a short route in easy countryside, on tracks and trails – the subject of off-trail navigation is covered in Chapter 4.

Actually, a compass can help even in easy country, so it's worth learning to use the compass no matter what sort of hiking you intend to do. The best way of navigating a route is to hike it in a series of short legs. Whenever you stop to navigate, use the following routine.

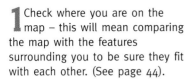

1 Check where you are on the map – this will mean comparing the map with the features surrounding you to be sure they fit with each other. (See page 44).

2 Decide the next point on your route to navigate to – as far as you can memorize the instructions to get there.

3 Read the map to turn into words the directions to the next point, using 'lefts' and 'rights' rather than 'north' or 'south'. You are creating your own guide book out of the map. Memorize the directions.

4 Follow the directions to walk the leg, enjoying the hike.

Try this method out using the piece of countryside around Rutter's Farm (see page 23).Your route is: first to Rutter's Farm and from there to take the trail over Windle Hill to the valley beyond.

Following the steps in 1–4 opposite:

● You know you are at the start of the farm track as you are clearly where the track meets the road. What's more, the countryside you can see ahead 'fits' with the symbols on the map.
● You will walk to Rutter's Farm as your next leg.
● You can read these instructions from the map: 'Walk along the farm track to the right-hand bend; here pick up the footpath left across the field to the farm.'
● Hike the leg. If you lose track of the directions as you go along, you should stop immediately and go through the process again, starting with 'Where are we now?'

In the directions we said 'to the right-hand bend'. Bends in tracks and trails show up very clearly on maps and give some of the best clues for telling where you are.

Sense of distance

This skill will help you to judge how far you have walked and will ring alarm bells if you walk beyond a difficult-to-see turning. You can build it up over a period of time on your hikes. To do this, take the trouble to estimate shorter and longer distances from where you are to objects you can see, and then measure those distances on the map. With time and practice, you will find you can do this without the map.

Chapter Four

Navigating off-trail: the compass

For many hikers the real challenge of the outdoors comes once they leave the safety of a well-trodden trail to break into wild country, but it is not a step to be taken lightly. A successful off-trail hike demands high standards of preparation, planning and, above all, navigation.

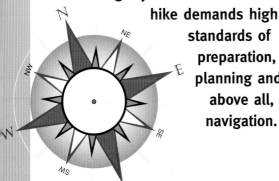

Off-trail

Off-trail there are fewer clues on the map to locate your position, putting much more reliance on contours, while the way ahead is more often obscured from sight by forest or mist. If you can see little more than a circle of mist, you quickly lose confidence about your current location. The map on its own is no longer enough to navigate by. This is where the compass comes in.

This simple device adds a vital extra clue to your route-finding, namely, direction. As will be explained, you can take a bearing from the map and use it to point on the ground the way to go. However, do not think if you master the compass then that is all you need to do; it is helpful only when used together with a high standard of map-reading.

Besides taking bearings, the other great job for a compass is to set the map (see page 44). While both bearings and setting the map are invaluable off-trail, do not think that they are not necessary when navigating along trails. They are a real helpmate then, and keep you in good practice for the rough-stuff.

How can a compass tell you which way to go? Underlying everything is the fact that the earth happens to be an enormous magnet, causing weak lines of magnetic force to lie everywhere on the earth's surface, pointing roughly from south to north. A freely suspended magnet (such as a compass needle) will always align itself with these lines of force, the red end of the needle pointing to magnetic north, thus providing a handy reference for any direction of travel.

The modern hiking compass is more than just a needle. It has a baseplate and dial to enable bearings to be taken from the map and then to be followed on the ground.

Precautions

● *Before taking your map out on a hike, check that it is overprinted with a reference grid. Failing this, you will have to draw carefully a series of north-south lines over your hiking area, spaced 4 cm/2 in. apart, parallel with the sides of the map.*
● *Attach your compass to your person or your map case – otherwise it is all too easy to lose it. You will need a longer cord than the one supplied with the compass.*
● *When using the compass, be sure there are no iron or steel objects nearby – these affect the magnetic needle. In some localities even the rock is magnetic, making a compass useless there. Be alert to this risk.*

Parts of the compass

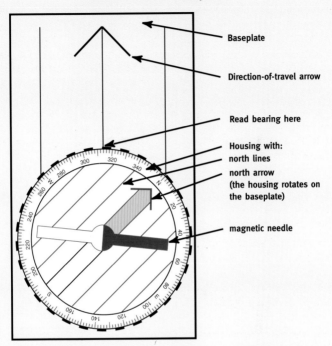

Baseplate

Direction-of-travel arrow

Read bearing here

Housing with:
north lines
north arrow
(the housing rotates on
the baseplate)

magnetic needle

This is a good stage to take a closer look at the essential components of a compass. Individual compasses may vary slightly in design, but all should have three main parts (as shown in the diagram above):

● *A **needle on a pivot**, whose*

magnetized red end always points to magnetic north, as we have seen.

● *The **circular housing** comes next. It's graduated in degrees on its edge (one graduation equals 2°) and contains a transparent centre with*

a north arrow — we shall see the use of this shortly.

● *Finally, note the **rectangular baseplate**. Its significant features are the edges of the plate and its direction-of-travel arrow.*

View from the clearing

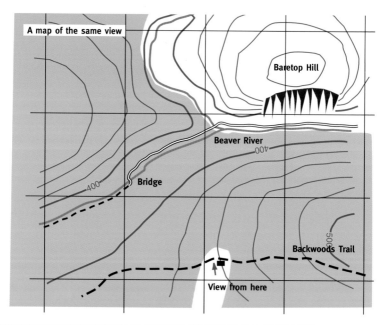

A map of the same view

Baretop Hill

Beaver River

400

Bridge

400

500

Backwoods Trail

View from here

Taking a bearing

Suppose that you have reached the clearing on the Backwoods Trail and now wish to cross the bridge over Beaver River. From there you would follow the track downstream.

On leaving the clearing you will be trekking through forest, so you will need a compass to point the direction to take.

There are two (possibly three) steps:

1 Take the bearing from the map and set it on the compass.

2 (Possibly: adjust the bearing for magnetic variation.)

3 Use the compass (set with bearing) to point the direction in the forest.

Step 1

Here you are working with the compass on the map. **You ignore the magnetic needle in this step.** Just follow the instructions in 1(a) below and 1(b) on page 40.

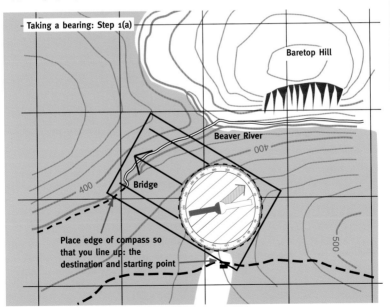

Taking a bearing: Step 1(a)

Baretop Hill

Beaver River

400

Bridge

400

500

Place edge of compass so that you line up: the destination and starting point

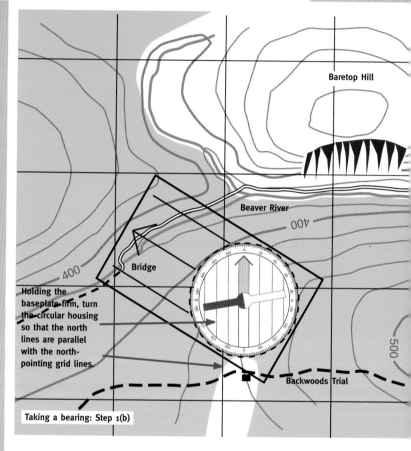

Holding the baseplate firm, turn the circular housing so that the north lines are parallel with the north-pointing grid lines.

Baretop Hill

Beaver River

Bridge

400

400

500

Backwoods Trial

Taking a bearing: Step 1(b)

Aiming Off

You may wonder why the bearing has been taken, not to the bridge itself, but off to the left. This technique, known as 'aiming off', is used when taking a bearing to a point on a linear feature (here a bridge on a river). If you aimed directly at the bridge, errors in following the bearing might bring you to the river out of sight of the bridge. Then you would not know whether to turn left or right. Doubt is avoided by aiming off on purpose to one side by, say, 10°. Thus, if you aim left, you know to turn right on reaching the river. You have now set your grid bearing on the map.

Step 2

Discover from the margin of the map what magnetic variation applies (look at the box opposite). If it is less than 5° (as in the UK) you can skip this step if you wish. If greater, you will have to shift the dial of the compass to adjust the bearing you have just captured:

● Direction of shift – anti-clockwise if magnetic variation is west, i.e. increase the bearing; and clockwise if east.
● Amount of shift – number of degrees of magnetic variation (each mark on the compass dial is 2°).

Magnetic variation

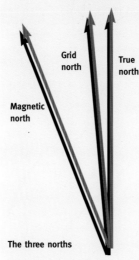

Grid north

True north

Magnetic north

The angle between grid and true north is usually so small that it may be ignored.

Example on map: Magnetic variation is 12° west, increasing by 1° in six years.

The three norths

The north lines of the grid on your map point near enough to true north; and these are the references against which the bearing in step 1 is taken. But the lines of magnetic force (which the needle will settle against in step 3) point to magnetic north. This is a different direction from true north in many parts of the world. The angle between magnetic north and true north is known as magnetic variation, magnetic angle or magnetic declination, and can be as large as 25°, more than enough to throw your bearing seriously off-course. The magnetic variation can be west or east of true north. Your map will have information in its margin about the magnetic variation that applies, possibly with a simple diagram such as the one above. It might also quote the annual change to the variation, so you can work out the current value from an old map.

The direction-of-travel arrow should always point directly away from you.

Step 3

Now you have the correct magnetic bearing on the compass. Put the map away and use the compass to point the direction to walk. It is during this part of the process that you are most likely to make an error, so it pays to do it carefully.

1 Hold the compass correctly (see photo, left).

2 Align the compass to point the way (see diagram, right).

3 Follow the bearing. If you cannot see your destination straight away, you will get there in short stages. With your compass aligned, carefully let your eye move up in the line of the direction of travel arrow to pick out a unique tree, rock or bush in the distance directly on this line. Then put your compass away, walk to that point, and stop again to repeat the process, until you reach your destination.

Align the compass to point the way.

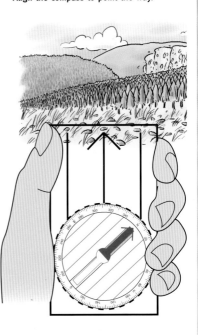

Turn your whole body to align the compass. The red end of the needle should be on the north arrow ('red on red').

Using bearings

Bearings taken in this way can also help when walking on trails. You are at a junction of tracks and do not know which one is yours. The compass, set with the bearing of the one you want, will point to the correct trail.

There are a number of compass techniques, but only one that is in common use.

This is 'setting the map' (explained in detail on page 44), which is an extremely useful skill to acquire, no matter where you are doing your map-reading.

Setting the map

Setting (or orienting) the map is to rotate it until it is aligned with the surrounding countryside. In this state, the trail you are standing on points in the same direction both on the ground and on the map; that hill over there is in the same direction on the map. The point of all this is that you can relate the map to the countryside much more easily with a set map than otherwise, to locate your position or seek out your next direction to take. And certainly when just starting to navigate, you should set the map each time you use it when out on the trail. Follow the three steps shown in the diagram on page 45.

1 Set a bearing of 360° on your compass, and adjust it for magnetic variation.

2 Hold the compass so that a long edge lies parallel with the edge of the map or a grid line.

3 Rotate map and compass together until the needle (red end) is aligned with the north arrow.

You will need to practise using a set map until it becomes second nature; at first you might feel awkward getting the set map in just the right position in front of you to compare the map with the piece of country you are interested in. Persevere, as the rewards of using a set map are immense. With time, and good contour interpretation added in, the map will seem to come alive and you will be able to link directly with what you see around you.

Attaching your compass

If you can find a way of attaching the compass permanently to the edge of the map as in the diagram opposite, inside your map case, you can free the hand that's holding it. Setting the map then becomes even easier to do.

You need to attach the compass as in the diagram opposite, with a clip replacing the thumb. Do not use a steel clip as it will influence the needle.

You can do all your compass work from a map set in this way. For example, to take a bearing of the direction of the next track you are going to follow:

● *Rotate the map so that the next track is pointing directly away from you, with your index finger on your current position.*

● *Hold the map firmly in this position, turn your whole body until the map is set. The direction of the track on the map points the way on the ground.*

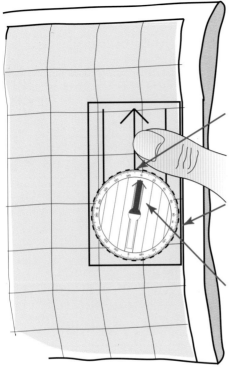

Step 1: Set the compass to magnetic variation (here it is 10° east).

Step 2: Align the compass baseplate with the edge of the map.

Step 3: Rotate the map and compass together so that the compass needle aligns with the north arrow.

Setting the map

Sense of direction

Unlike homing pigeons, humans do not have any in-built sense of direction, but by being aware of your wider surroundings as you walk, you can check out your detailed navigation decisions to avoid the worst mistakes. Before setting out, form a mental image of the shape of your route, set against the large features you will see as you go. Then you will know for example that a certain hill should be kept to the right in the early part of the hike. If you see it in another direction you know to double-check your map-reading.

Chapter Five

Planning a route

Previous chapters have set
out the basics of map-reading
and navigating a hike.
The knowledge you have
gained from them must be
put to one other crucial task
– planning your hike.

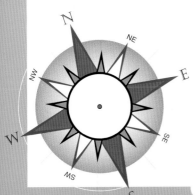

Basic planning

Anything more than a two-hour hike in easy country should be organized with some care, especially if it leaves the safety of recognized trails for dangerous or rough terrain. Poor planning might lead, at best, to arriving back late and exhausted, and at worst an unexpected night out, getting lost in hostile territory, or injury to one of your party.

There are three basic steps:

1 Decide your aims and choose a possible route.

2 Check the route out (adjust and recheck until you are satisfied with it).

3 Make a route card and inform a responsible person before setting out.

Setting your aims

First you must decide what you want from the hike. Do you have some special reason for wanting to do this particular hike? How long should it be, in distance and time? Should you keep to trails or go into back country? What options do you have for start and finish points? Bear in mind the needs of all your party.

Choosing a route

All your imagination and map knowledge are brought into play in coming up with a satisfying route. You scan the map of your chosen area and look for a line of likely trails which connect to make a hike that seems to meet your aims. All the time you should be visualizing what the route will be like to walk. You will look at the contours to find good views, and also to make sure the route is not too steep or dangerous. Take note of the forests – do you want to walk through them or bypass them?

Off-trail routes

Choosing a route off-trail calls for something extra and you will need to check whether it is easy to navigate. Not having the comforting line of a trail, you want as far as possible to find other natural lines to follow, such as a hill ridge or the edge of a forest. These are known as 'handrails' (look at the diagram opposite). If you do need to take a compass bearing to traverse a featureless area, make sure it ends with a clearly defined feature, such as a stream, lying across your path – known as 'collecting features' – to be sure of your location when you get there. The collecting feature could even become a handrail for the next part of the route. Check your route against the contours to be sure there are no needless ascents and descents.

Often a longer route, for example one skirting the head of a valley, is more pleasant and might even be quicker than the direct way into and out of a valley.

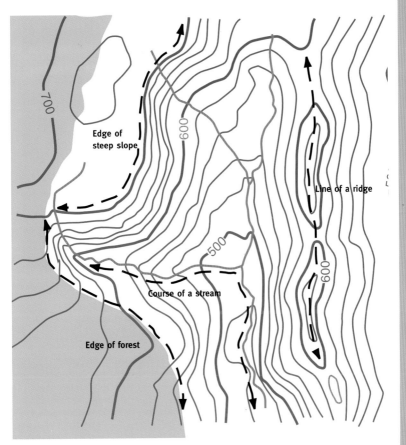

Examples of handrails – natural lines in the landscape, which are easy to follow.

Check out the route

You must look at the route critically to be certain it meets its aims and can be managed by your party. Check it out for steepness, streams that may have to be crossed, alternative or escape routes that could be used if the weather turned nasty. If you are not happy, you will need to make adjustments until you are.

Allow extra time for rough or difficult ground.

- *The most critical check is for distance and time. If you have no wheeled map-measurer, you can use a piece of string to lay along the route, matching all its wiggles. Stretch it out along the map's scale bar (or over the grid squares, if you know how far they are spaced) to read the distance.*

- *To convert to walking time, you need to know how fast you will walk. A good pace for a fit party on the level in easy terrain is an average of 5 km/3 miles per hour. In practice this is rarely achieved so you would be wise to use a lower figure, say 4 km. Even this figure must be reduced for heavy loads, snow, mud, or off-trail walking. So, if your hike measures 12 km and you are assuming a speed of 3 km per hour, you allow four hours, for the level walking time.*

- *To this you must add an allowance if there is climbing to be done (check out the contours for this). The usual rule of thumb is to*

add an extra 30 minutes for every 300 m/1000 ft of ascent.

- *Also add an extra two hours for a day hike to take into account breaks: 15 minutes each for morning and afternoon breaks, 45 minutes lunch and 45 minutes contingency.*

- *Does the total walking time let you get back in time?*

ROUTE CARD

Day of week SAT	**Date** 20/7/2000	

NAMES OF GROUP MEMBERS
Alison Furnell, Fiona Smith
Azam Khan, Johnny Faulkner

NAME OF GROUP Apex Youth
Address 246 Main Street
Anytown

Setting out time 1000

Tel: 088-99 00 99 00

Start Backwoods Trail car park on HWY 93 GR 383731

LEG	PLACE WITH GRID REFERENCE	General direction of bearing	Distance in km/miles	Height climbed in m/ft	Time allowed for leg	Time for stops and meals	Total time for leg	Estimated or arrival (ETA)	Details of route for leg	Escape to:
1	TO Hut/clearing 322742	W	6.2k	400m	2h10m	15m	2h25m	1225	Backwoods Trail to clearing	Return
2	TO Bridge over Beaver River 310751	NW	1.5k	–	30m	45m	1 h15m	1340	Bearing of 300° grid (312° mag)	Return
3	TO Baretop Hill 332765	NE	3k	50m	50m	–	50m	1430	Track to second bridge, then bearing of 62° magnetic	Track to HWY 93
4	TO Carpark on HWY 93 383731	SE	5.5k	–	1 h20m	15m	1 h35m	1605	Descend on bearing of 132° mag. then track to HWY 93, turn right	Track to HWY 93
5	TO									
6	TO									
	TOTALS:		1 6.2k	450m	4h 50m	1 h15m	6h 05m		**Bad weather alternative** Walk out on Backwoods Trail, return same way	

As an extra precaution, prepare a detailed route card to leave with a responsible person.

Preparing a route card

As a final piece of preparation, it is always wise to make out two copies of a route card (see above), leaving one with a responsible person, who can raise the alarm if you do not return in good time. This means you must let this person know when you have returned safely, or they will raise the alarm unnecessarily!

Routes for later

An excellent habit to develop on your hikes is to be constantly on the lookout for paths or other routes that seem 'goers' for future use. You may spot them in the distance, on the other side of the valley, or up in the mountains. Perhaps, as you slowly climb a hillside in the morning, you can see across the valley the details of the best way to make the descent you have planned for the end of the route. Or you may see a splendid trail or hill-ridge that would make a fine hike another day. Store these nuggets away in your memory bank.

Chapter Six

Emergencies

By its nature as a challenging activity, hiking carries somewhat more risk of accident than crossing the street in the city. And because the hiker is dependent on what he carries with him, remote from modern services, he is less well placed than the city-dweller to cope with misfortune, if it occurs.

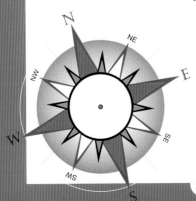

Most incidents in practice are minor, easily dealt with in a few minutes, and hardly affect the course of a hike. More seldom, a serious incident will occur, ranging from a twisted ankle to a fatal accident.

These notes look at the more common types of incident and what to do if an emergency arises.

For longer or more hazardous expeditions, a tent is essential.

Lost!

Finding yourself in the fix that you cannot pinpoint your position on the map might well be the most common type of emergency. It happens when you lose concentration, come across terrain difficult to navigate, or visibility fails due to mist, tree cover or darkness. What should you do? The main point is to stay as calm as possible, don't panic and try to look at your situation as logically as you can.

Here is a three-step plan:

1 Maybe you do know where you are, after all. Compare the map with the location about you more closely than you have done so far.

2 If step 1 fails, could you retrace your steps to return to somewhere you recognize, and replan your route from there?

3 If all else fails, you may have to spend the night outside.
If you decide you have to move – could you at least define an area in which you might be, even quite a large one?

Accident procedure

Suppose a member of your party has twisted or broken an ankle, or is beginning to suffer serious hypothermia. Clearly the hike cannot be continued. Your two priorities are to go for help and to make the injured person comfortable.

Getting help

Without a mobile phone, a party member (two if possible) will have to set off to the nearest road or telephone to alert the rescue services. Be sure to take a note of the location (grid reference) of the incident, and the nature of the injuries. Telephone the general emergency services, who will contact specialized mountain rescue if necessary. Once the rescue party is making its way towards you on foot, you will want to attract it to the injured person (or if you want to attract another party), use the international rescue call on your whistle – six three-second blasts, repeated once a minute.

Making the injured person comfortable

Once a person stops walking, they can become cold very quickly. Try to maintain body temperature by following these steps:

1 Find or construct a sheltered place.

2 Dress the casualty as warmly as possible.

3 Put the injured person in a plastic survival bag.

4 Make the insulation layer under the casualty as warm and watertight as possible.

Think like this

We could not have walked as far as this stream, and I am sure we have got beyond that level shelf.' Then work out a direction to take (perhaps aiming for a linear feature such as a road) which will be safe, no matter where you are in your area of probability.

Remember

Do not call out the rescue services unless strictly necessary. Bear in mind that some countries charge for providing rescue services. If that is the case, you may want to consider taking out a good insurance policy that would meet the cost of these charges.

First-aid kit

It is a wise precaution for someone in the party to carry a first-aid kit (and to know how to use it). A simple personal kit could contain the following:

- *Assorted plasters*
- *Blister dressings*
- *Triangular bandage*
- *Safety pins*
- *Crepe bandage*
- *Scissors*
- *Tweezers*

- *Tubigrip elasticated bandage*
- *Sterile wound dressings*
- *Antiseptic wipes*
- *Adhesive wound-binding strips*
- *Micropore tape*
- *Rubber gloves*
- *Common brand pain tablets*

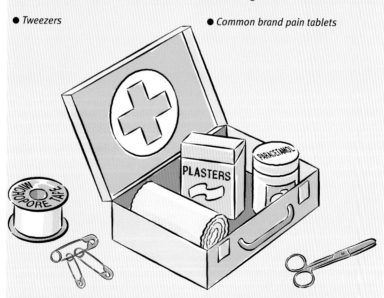

First aid

These notes give only a brief summary of basic first-aid techniques, insufficient on their own to ensure competence. There is no substitute for attending a recognized course. Here are the common techniques, the more serious first:

Resuscitation

If a casualty loses consciousness, you must check for a pulse (the carotid artery in the neck) and breathing (look at the chest). If either seem to be failing, the brain is not receiving its proper oxygen supply, so action is needed within three minutes. The most urgent priority is to seek medical assistance. While waiting for this, apply first aid. Lie the casualty on his back (taking great care if back injury is also suspected) and follow the 'A,B,C' routine outlined below and on pp 58–59.

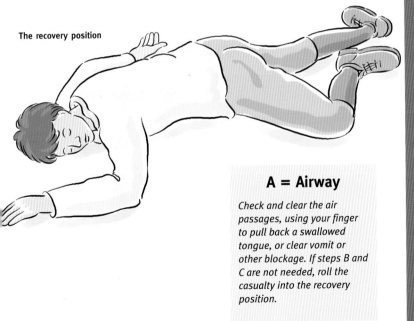

The recovery position

A = Airway

Check and clear the air passages, using your finger to pull back a swallowed tongue, or clear vomit or other blockage. If steps B and C are not needed, roll the casualty into the recovery position.

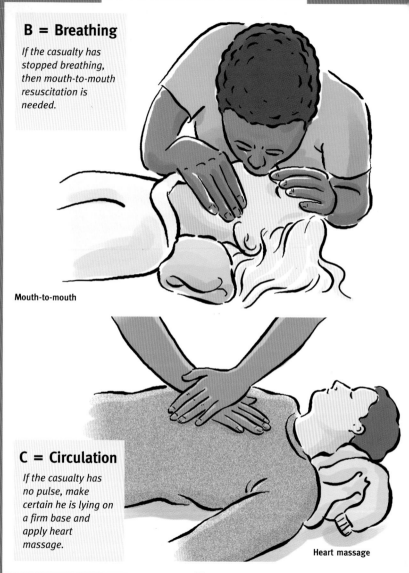

B = Breathing

If the casualty has stopped breathing, then mouth-to-mouth resuscitation is needed.

Mouth-to-mouth

C = Circulation

If the casualty has no pulse, make certain he is lying on a firm base and apply heart massage.

Heart massage

Head injury

If the casualty is vomiting, check that the air passages are clear and roll him into the recovery position. Check how aware and alert he is, and in the case of marked deterioration, seek medical assistance as a matter of urgency.

Bleeding

Apply pressure directly on the wound, using a clean pad of cloth, but avoid applying so much pressure that the blood supply is cut off from extremities. If no cloth is available your fingers will do. Keep the pressure up as long as is necessary for the flow to stop. The flow of blood from a wound can be reduced dramatically by raising the wound above the level of the rest of the body.

Spinal injury

If the casualty is unable to move arms or legs, complains about shooting pains down the back or limbs, or has areas of numbness or pins and needles, then suspect spinal injury. DO NOT MOVE the casualty, unless to save life. Seek urgent medical assistance. If the casualty must be moved to save life, do so as carefully as possible, on as rigid a platform as can be devised.

Torn muscles, tendons and ligaments

These injuries are helped by:

● Rest – to prevent aggravating the injury.

● Strapping up – to improve the circulation in the affected area.

● Elevation – to reduce swelling.

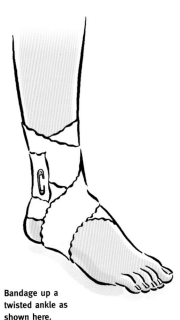

Bandage up a twisted ankle as shown here.

Fractures and dislocation

Unless there are complications such as trapped blood vessels, medical treatment is not usually needed before the casualty reaches hospital. First aid should be directed at immobilizing the fracture to prevent pain from movement. Use bandages and such splints as can be improvised. Arm fractures can be supported in a sling, possibly strapping the limb to the body. Leg fractures can often be better immobilized if the two legs are strapped together to a firm structure.

Hypothermia

If conditions are conducive to people getting chilled (wet, windy cold), and a member of the party seems confused, uncoordinated or overly tired, hypothermia can be suspected. With this, the core of the person's body cools below its normal temperature. To prevent it, wear suitable outdoor clothing, keep well protected from the elements and maintain adequate high-energy food intake.

Hypothermia is best treated by creating dry and warm conditions for the individual, using any spare clothing available. If the casualty is too exhausted to continue, you should improvize shelter – study the details under 'Accident Procedure' (page 55).

Severe hypothermia requires urgent skilled medical assistance.

Burns and scalds

Cool the affected area for about ten minutes, then cover with a sterile dry dressing. If the burns are deep, seek skilled medical assistance as soon as possible.

Sunburn and sunstroke

Sunburn is all too common; it is easy to underestimate the power of the sun's ultraviolet rays. It can be prevented by simple measures to protect the skin: wearing a suitable hat and clothing, and using a high-factor sunblock cream. The only treatment for sunburn is to apply a soothing lotion, such as calamine, to the affected area.

Sunstroke is a very different problem. It is caused by overexertion in high temperatures and aggravated by humid conditions, with too little water intake. Sunstroke can be serious and requires immediate action, preferably under medical supervision. The casualty should rest in the shade, drink water, and be cooled as effectively as possible.

Wear a hat with a brim, sensible clothing and a high-factor sunblock cream to protect yourself from the fierce rays of the sun.

Useful addresses

Organizations
There are far too many local clubs to list, and you can easily get the relevant details from your library or information centre. Here are some of the major organizations.

United Kingdom
Ramblers' Association
1/5 Wandsworth Road
London SW8 2XX
Tel: 0171 339 8500
e-mail: ramblers@london.
ramblers.org.uk

Long-Distance Walkers' Assoc.
C/o Les Maple
21 Upcroft
Windsor
Berks SL4 3NH
Tel: 01753 866685
The many sections of the LDWA organize a programme of long hikes for those wishing to test their powers of endurance.

British Orienteering Federation
Riversdale
Dale Road North
Darley Dale, Matlock
Derbyshire
DE4 2HX
Tel: 01629 734042
Fax: 01629 733769

The British Orienteering Foundation has many local clubs and organizes regular events.

Australia
National Parks Association
PO Box A96
Sydney South
NSW 1235
e-mail: npansw@bigpond.com
web: http://www.bushwalking
.org.au

Confederation of Bushwalking Clubs, New South Wales
GPO Box 2090
Sydney 1043
Tel: (02) 929 46797
e-mail: turton@fastlink.com.au
web: http://www.bushwalking.org.au

Canberra Bushwalking Club
PO Box 160
Canberra ACT 2601
Tel: (02) 6288 7863
web: http://www.pcug.org.au

USA
American Hiking Society
PO Box 20160
Washington DC
200041-2160
e-mail: AmHiker@aol.com
web: http://ahs.simplenet.com

Other information

The YHA runs a chain of hostels and camping barns, mostly in the countryside, providing its members with very reasonably-priced accommodation. Members tend to come from younger age groups. The YHA also offers courses on navigation and hiking.

English Youth Hostels Association
Trevelyan House
8 St Stephen's Hill
St Albans
Herts AL1 2DY
Tel: 01727 855215

Scottish Youth Hostels Association
7 Glebe Crescent
Stirling
FK8 2JA
Tel: 01786 451181

Australian Youth Hostel Association
GPO Box 5276
Sydney
NSW 2001
Tel: 612 9261 111

Outdoor equipment suppliers

As there are shops selling outdoor equipment and clothing in every town and city, a full list would be impossible to provide. In the UK good suppliers with stores nationwide are Blacks (Tel: 0191 5182002) and the YHA shops. High-quality outdoor clothing is also available by mail order from companies such as Hawkshead, which advertize regularly in the national newspapers.

In Australia look out for:
Paddy Pallin
74 Macquarie Street
Parramatta
NSW 2150
Tel: 612 9633 1113

Alsport
1045 Victoria Road
West Ryde
NSW 2114
Tel: 612 9858 5844

Index